W9-AHJ-667

DATE DUE

DEC 07 1989	APR 28 1990		

DEMCO 38-297

EVELYN CISNEROS
Prima Ballerina

EVELYN CISNEROS
Prima Ballerina

By Charnan Simon

 CHILDRENS PRESS®

CHICAGO

PHOTO CREDITS

Courtesy Cisneros family — 5, 7 (2 photos), 8 (2 photos), 9, 10 (2 photos), 11, 12 (3 photos), 14, 15
Courtesy San Francisco Ballet — 17, 20, 23, 30; © Lloyd Englert, 3, 31; © Gary Sinick, 19; © Bonnie Kamin, cover
© Marty Sohl — 1, 2, 6, 21, 22 (2 photos), 24, 25, 26, 27, 28, 32

Project Editor: E. Russell Primm III
Design: Biner Design
Photo Research: Judy Feldman

Library of Congress Cataloging-in-Publication Data

Simon, Charnan.
    Evelyn Cisneros : Prima Ballerina / by Charnan Simon.
        p.   cm. — (A picture story biography)
    Summary: Describes the early life, training, and accomplishments of the Mexican American dancer who is the prima ballerina for the San Francisco Ballet.
    ISBN 0-516-04276-9
    1. Cisneros, Evelyn, 1958- — Juvenile literature. 2. Ballet dancers—United States—Biography—Juvenile literature. 3. Ballerinas—United States—Biography—Juvenile literature. [1. Cisneros, Evelyn, 1958- . 2. Ballet dancers. 3. Mexican Americans—Biography.] I. Title. II. Series.

GV1785.C57S58 1990   [92]90-40104
[B]   CIP
                                                                  AC

As the curtain fell, the audience rose to its feet, clapping wildly. The San Francisco Ballet had just finished a performance of *Sleeping Beauty*. The princess found her prince and lived happily ever after. The audience, however, wasn't ready to let their princess go.

"Brava!" they shouted, throwing flowers to the stage. "Brava! Brava!"

The curtains rose, and Sleeping Beauty herself came to the center of

Evelyn Cisneros in the ballet *Sleeping Beauty*.

the stage. She bowed gracefully and smiled. Evelyn Cisneros looked exactly like a princess.

Evelyn Cisneros is the prima ballerina for the San Francisco Ballet. She has danced on stages around the world. It is hard to imagine that she was once so shy she wouldn't even talk in school.

Evelyn Cisneros was born in Long Beach, California, on November 18, 1958. The Cisneros family soon

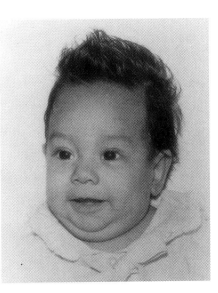

Evelyn at three months of age (above), and with her younger brother Robert.

Evelyn and Robert at a family wedding
(left), and a picture taken with their
mother.

moved to the seaside town of
Huntington Beach. Evelyn, her
younger brother Robert, and her
parents were a warm and close-knit
family. They were also the only
Mexican-American family in
Huntington Beach for a long time.
Evelyn's father was a precision
machinist whose parents had come to
America from Mexico as migrant

workers. Evelyn's mother's family had come to the United States from Durango, Mexico, in 1910 after the outbreak of the Mexican Revolution.

Belonging to such a loving family helped when neighborhood children teased Evelyn about how "different" she looked. Evelyn's dark skin, hair, and eyes made her stand out from her friends. Evelyn grew more and more timid. By the time she was seven, she was afraid to even raise her hand or speak out in class.

Evelyn's first performance modeling at a local mall.

Evelyn's first ballet solo at age 8 1/2
(left), and her first toe dance at age 9.

Evelyn's mother thought perhaps dance classes would help cure her daughter's shyness. At first, Evelyn didn't like ballet class. She remembers, "I was very shy, and it was hard for me to stand in front of everyone in tights and leotard."

Evelyn's mother encouraged her to go to class for at least a year. By the end of the year, Evelyn had met Phyllis Cyr, who would be her first real ballet teacher. Phyllis Cyr taught Evelyn how to enjoy ballet. She showed Evelyn how to move to different kinds of music and to see the beauty of dance.

Evelyn worked hard at being a good dancer. She was naturally graceful, and turns and jumps came easily to her. But her left foot turned slightly inward, and Evelyn worked hours on stretching exercises to get the foot to turn out.

Evelyn and Robert Cisneros perform a tap dance.

While in junior high school Evelyn performed a wide variety of roles and danced both ballet and tap.

Then, too, Evelyn's shoulders were naturally somewhat rounded. Again, Evelyn worked many long hours to develop flexibility and strength in her shoulders and back.

Hard work didn't bother Evelyn. With her family's support, Evelyn learned all that she could about dance. And not just ballet, either. Evelyn quickly mastered jazz, tap, and other styles of dancing.

Dance lessons were expensive, and for a long time the Cisneros family could afford only one class a week. To help pay for more lessons, Evelyn taught tap dancing and demonstrated ballet positions for younger students. Mrs. Cisneros helped, too, by working at the front desk of the dance studio.

By the time she was fourteen, Evelyn knew she had a decision to make. She was enjoying school. In

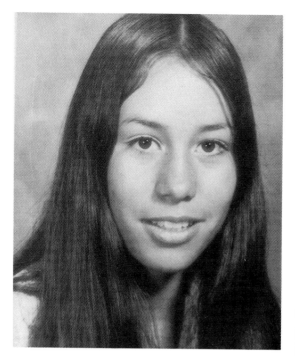

Evelyn's eighth grade school picture.

junior high she played softball, basketball, and volleyball—and held the long distance track record for her school district. Evelyn knew it would be hard to give up her school activities and devote herself to ballet. But it would be even harder to give up ballet. Evelyn chose dance.

From 7:30 in the morning until 2:30 in the afternoon, Evelyn went to junior high with her friends. After school she headed straight to the ballet studio. All afternoon she attended ballet class, demonstrated steps for other teachers, and taught tap class herself. After a quick dinner at home, she would go to the Pacific Ballet Theatre in Los Angeles. Evelyn danced at least five nights a week.

When she was fourteen, Evelyn's dance teachers encouraged her to try

Evelyn Cisneros, a mature 17-year-old high-school senior.

out for the San Francisco Ballet School. The teachers in San Francisco were impressed by Evelyn. To her surprise and delight, she was offered a full scholarship for the summer session.

Evelyn thrived under her new challenge. She practiced new and harder steps, and began acting some of the characters from famous ballets. More and more Evelyn was convinced that this was where she was meant to be.

The next year both the San Francisco Ballet School and the School of American Ballet in New York City offered Evelyn scholarships for their summer sessions. As much as she had loved San Francisco, Evelyn and her parents thought she should go to New York.

The summer proved to be scary, exciting—and disappointing. Fifteen-year-old Evelyn had never been away from her family for so long. She had never lived in such a huge, confusing city as New York. Still, she looked forward to studying with some of the finest dancers in the world. But when ballet school started, Evelyn was put in a very slow class. Evelyn recalls, "By the end of the summer, I was very

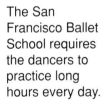

The San Francisco Ballet School requires the dancers to practice long hours every day.

discouraged. I felt very depressed, and so unsure of the talent I had that I was just about ready to quit dancing."

Evelyn's parents again helped. They suggested that she call the San Francisco Ballet School. The company invited her to join them for the last week of their summer session and to come back the following summer as well.

Evelyn worked hard at school all winter and returned to San Francisco the summer she was sixteen. At the end of that summer, the company offered to make her an apprentice. This would mean she would have to move to San Francisco and dance full time. At the end of the year, if she were good enough, she would be invited to join the company.

On February 1, 1976, Evelyn Cisneros moved to San Francisco. Within a year, she had joined the company as a full-fledged member of the ballet. She was just eighteen years old.

Evelyn quickly attracted the attention of the company's artistic director, Michael Smuin. In 1979 he created a major role for her in his ballet titled *A Song for Dead Warriors*. This ballet was broadcast nationally and turned out to be very controversial.

Evelyn Cisneros and Antonio Lopez in the world premiere of *A Song for Dead Warriors*.

The ballet told about the mistreatment of Native Americans. Some people loved the ballet, and others hated it. Critics everywhere, however, praised Evelyn Cisneros's dancing ability.

In 1980, while the company was performing in New York City, the leading ballerina was injured. Evelyn was called on to take her place. Important writers from newspapers and magazines saw her dance and praised her performance. Almost overnight

Evelyn Cisneros and dancers from the San Francisco Ballet perform for President and Mrs. Reagan in the White House.

Evelyn portrays Juliet in *Romeo and Juliet*. Russell Murphy is her Romeo.

Evelyn Cisneros became a very famous dancer.

Triumph followed triumph in the next few years. In 1981, Evelyn again appeared on television in the ballet *The Tempest*. In 1982, she danced both ballet and tap in a live telecast from the White House. Later that same year, she received more praise from both audiences and critics for her lead role in a new version of *Romeo and Juliet*.

Not everything went smoothly for the young ballerina, however. In 1978, when she was just nineteen, she married fellow dancer David McNaughton. Less than two years later, Evelyn and David were divorced. It was a sad time. Evelyn's close family hadn't prepared her for a personal upset such as this.

There were professional upsets as well. In 1985, Michael Smuin was replaced by Helgi Tomasson as

Helgi Tomasson, artistic director of the San Francisco Ballet, oversees rehearsals of *Sleeping Beauty* with Evelyn and Anthony Randazzo.

Helgi Tomasson

director of the San Francisco Ballet.
During his years in San Francisco,
Smuin had worked closely with
Evelyn. He had created some of his
finest roles for her, and she had grown
under his direction.

Helgi Tomasson, however, also
appreciated Evelyn's talent and her
popularity as a leading ballerina. He
has continued to give her important

A performance of *Swan Lake*.

roles and has even created two new
ballets especially for her. "In the
beginning it was very difficult,"
Evelyn admits. "But now we have a
very reliable working relationship."

Evelyn Cisneros has truly earned the
title of prima ballerina. One night she
is the lovely, playful Princess Aurora

in *Sleeping Beauty*. The next night she dazzles in the double role of Odette/Odile in *Swan Lake*. She shows off her brilliant technique in difficult modern ballets, and sparkles as the Sugar Plum Fairy in the Christmas favorite, *The Nutcracker Suite*.

Evelyn dances the role of Sleeping Beauty. Prince Charming is performed by Anthony Randazzo.

Evelyn's dark Hispanic beauty, which was once a source of childhood teasing, is now admired by audiences everywhere. Today, Evelyn Cisneros is an international dancing star; she has never forgotten her roots. Evelyn is proud of her cultural heritage. Young Hispanics look up to her as an inspiration. She takes her

Evelyn Cisneros dances a scene from *LaFille Mal Gardée* with Jim Sohm.

Evelyn Cisneros
and Jean Charles
Gil in a ballet,
called *Rubies*,
created by
George
Balanchine.

responsibilities as a spokesperson for
the Hispanic community seriously.

Evelyn Cisneros has received
awards from Hispanic Women Making
History in 1984 and the Mexican
American Legal Defense Fund in 1985.
In 1987, she was honored as an
outstanding member of the Hispanic

The San Francisco Ballet production of *Swan Lake*.

community by the National Concilio of America. The next year, in 1988, she was honored for her outstanding achievement in the performing arts by the California State League of United Latin American Citizens. That same year she also was a spokesperson for a Latino youth conference held at California State University.

Evelyn also talks often to school children about what her life is like. She tells young dancers, "When you do anything athletic—and ballet is very hard on your body—you have to take good care of yourself. You have to make sure you eat properly and get enough rest."

When Evelyn is not dancing she and her husband, former dancer Robert Sund, share their home with two cats, Chatito and Boris. They like to walk on the beach, invite friends over for dinner, and go to the movies. For vacations, she and Robert go to Hawaii, or to visit Evelyn's parents in Baja, California.

Evelyn Cisneros has traveled a long way from being a shy little Mexican-American girl in Huntington Beach. Today, she is comfortable on dance stages around the world. Instead of

Former-dancer Robert Sund is married to Evelyn Cisneros.

A scene from the ballet *Theme and Variations*, which is danced to music by Tchaikovsky and was created by George Balanchine.

being teased and left out, she is applauded wherever she goes. Through hard work and determination, she has turned her talent into a treasure.

EVELYN CISNEROS

1958	November 18—Born in Long Beach, California, oldest of two children
1968	First ballet solo and first toe dance solo
1976	Moved to San Francisco to dance with San Francisco Ballet
1979	Danced starring role in *A Song for Dead Warriors*
1980	Steps into starring role in New York City after leading ballerina is injured; newspapers and magazines write glowing reviews
1981	Evelyn Cisneros appears on national television in the ballet *The Tempest*
1982	Dances for President and Mrs. Reagan at the White House; performance is broadcast nationally on PBS
1982	Evelyn receives praise from critics and audiences for leading role in new version of *Romeo and Juliet*
1984	Evelyn Cisneros receives award from Hispanic Women Making History
1985	Receives award from Mexican American Legal Defense Fund
1985	Helgi Tomasson appointed Artistic Director of San Francisco Ballet
1987	Honored as outstanding member of Hispanic community by the National Concilio of America
1988	Honored for outstanding achievement in the performing arts by the California State League of United Latin American Citizens
1990	Evelyn Cisneros dances the leading role in a new version of *Sleeping Beauty* created by Helgi Tomasson

INDEX

ABOUT THE AUTHOR

Charnan Simon grew up in Ohio, Georgia, Oregon, and Washington. She holds a B.A. degree in English Literature from Carleton College in Northfield, Minnesota, and an M.A. in English Literature from the University of Chicago. She worked for children's trade book companies after college and became the managing editor of *Cricket* magazine before beginning her career as a free-lance writer. Ms. Simon has written dozens of books and articles for young people and especially likes writing—and reading—history, biography, and fiction of all sorts. She lives in Chicago with her husband and two daughters.